NINE A.M. COFFEE, TEA, OR SNOOZE:

A SIMPLE APPROACH TO FINDING THE RIGHT JOB

LUCY CAPUL

Table of Contents

CHAPTER ONE: WHO "DIS"?...1
CHAPTER TWO: LET'S GET IN PAPER FORMATION.......................................9
CHAPTER THREE: MAKE MONEY MOVES 15

Introduction

It is nine a.m., early Monday morning. This is a time that a majority of professionals can relate to. This is the time you sip your first cup of coffee, the moment you walk into your office, or your first scheduled meeting of the day. The question is: Is this your favorite part of the day?

Nine A.M. was composed to help students, recent college graduates, or even current professionals focus and/or refocus themselves in their career search and make sure they are on the correct path. Finding your dream job is a job in itself that many young professionals in today's climate are struggling with. The team at *AffordableCollegePrep* has come together to make this guide outlining an easy process to help you get your dream job.

It's Nine A.M. Coffee, Tea, or Snooze?

CHAPTER ONE: WHO "DIS"?

 ## Introduction:

Welcome to Chapter 1 of Nine A.M. Regardless of whatever stage you are at in life, this workbook can help. Searching for the next career opportunity can be difficult if you do not have the right resources. This workbook is here to provide you with the tools you need to be on the right path, providing a concierge-like service to ensure you are succeeding in your career's development.

Each chapter is designed as a career hunt checklist with specific notes to help you along the way. Go through all of the steps and check each step off, once completed. There are "sticky notes" in some sections for you to jot down notes. For direct access to our Career Development Advisor, please purchase the complete Career Development Package on the affordable college prep website which includes personalized services like proofreading resumes and additional advising via email.

We are here to help you succeed in your career search. Let's get started!

Brainstorming

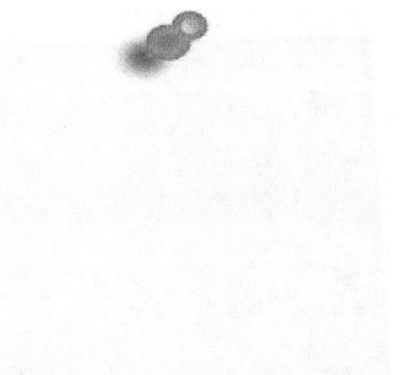

Let's brainstorm together! Which one are you? Use the sticky note on the right to start brainstorming.

Are you in the process of graduating college or you a recent college graduate?

Are you in the middle of your career and want a career change? Why do you seek a career change?

What industry are you searching for careers in? What type of positions are you looking for (hourly, contract, management, etc.)?

Career Objectives

Brainstorm some ideas about your career development goals for the future and what you want. This step is essential in making sure you are on the right path to success. You do not want to be stuck in a job that you do not enjoy or be in the position where you find yourself switching jobs from year to year. This will hurt your career and it does not look promising when potential hiring managers look at your resume. Take a moment to answer the questions below.

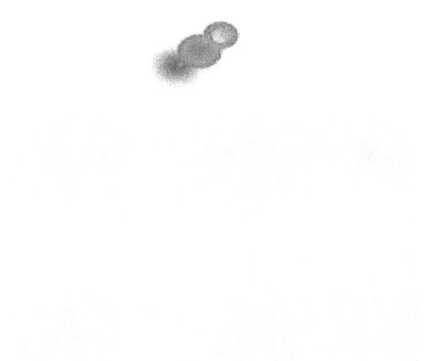

- What are your career goals within the next 5-10 years?
- Think about the specific positions that you are applying for and if there are possibilities of growth within that position or company. Look at the company's website, as well as their mission and vision statements. Do your research!

- What is your ultimate goal? Do you want to climb the ladder for the next 5-10 years to gain enough experience to eventually own your business?

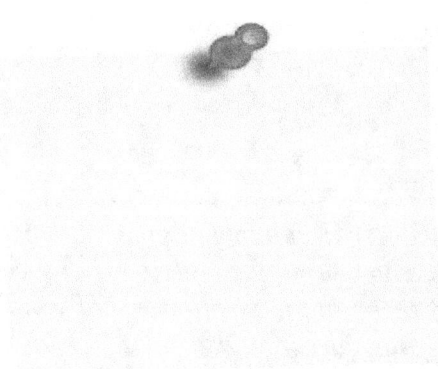

- Do you want to be in a management role (more hours) or be comfortable within a non-leadership position?

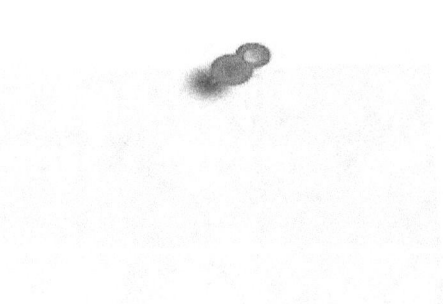

Now that we have brainstormed your career objectives, let's dive into your personal objectives.

☐ Personal Objectives

Brainstorm some ideas about your personal development and goals, as well and how that may affect your career timeline. Life happens but it is always great to brainstorm some ideas on what you want in life so that your career and personal goals are not conflicted.

Are you a recent college graduate and want to focus on paying your loans and becoming financially stable within the next 5 years? What are your financial plans?

Are you thinking of settling down and starting a family?

Already have a family? If you are in the middle of a career change, will it affect your personal life? Are you able to balance both a career and a family? We want to make sure you are not overwhelmed.

Thinking of going back to school or a special program? Thinking of applying to graduate school? Have you checked out our video on the cost of applying to graduate school? Visit our Videos page and check out "The Real Cost of a Master's Degree".

Now that we have discussed your career and personal goals, it's time to start building your brand for you to start your job search. Are you ready?

Creating Your Brand

Creating your personal brand is important in career development. The use of social media is very important in our generation as it brands an individual and can also lead to potential full time positions.

> ➢ **LinkedIn**
> If you do not have a LinkedIn account, what are you waiting for? It is a free online website that builds your personal networking profile online. Think of it as a professional version of Facebook. Go to www.linkedin.com and sign up. Don't worry, we will take you step by step in building your profile below. Let's get started!

Profile Photo: Make sure you have a professional profile photo. This is not Facebook or Instagram. If you do not have one, you can easily take one with your phone and capture a headshot image. Wear clothing that you would wear in your industry. Most hiring managers will not look at someone's profile if they do not have a profile image. Remember you are branding yourself.

Cover Photo: This is optional. But this will add to your brand. If you work for a   company, are in school, part of an organization, or are living in one of largest cities in the world, place a photo that depicts who you may represent and that, in turn, represents you. If you spoke at an event, place that photo as your cover photo. It will attract hiring managers to your profile and get them to read about your background.

Headline: This is an area for you to place your industry, your current position, or if you are looking for a specific position/positions. LinkedIn has changed over the years; there is now a section that allows you to share if you are seeking work or provide consulting services. Be smart about your headline. Make sure it is a concise version of your elevator speech or your brand. Make sure to place your industry. For example, if you have different experiences in higher education, but not necessarily teaching, you can market yourself as a "Higher Education Professional." This will persuade similar professionals to click on your profile and read about your experience and see if you are seeking a career in higher education and what experiences you may have had.

Work Experience: Make sure to list your work experience as accurately as possible. Make sure to include and link the companies that you worked for or in. Treat this as your online resume. Make sure to write your accomplishments. Hiring managers don't want to know what a "Marketing Manager" does because they already know. They want to know what you have _contributed_ to your company. This will portray you as a valuable member and asset to their company, which might lead to potential job opportunities. Outline specifics, such as the number of staff you managed on a daily basis or the amount of revenue you brought in per quarter.

Volunteer Experience & Organizations: This is a chance for hiring managers to see you as an individual. Share any clubs, organizations, and/or volunteer experiences you participated in. Remember, hiring managers want to hire a person that can contribute to the wellbeing of their company, not a robot. Include organizations that you are active in or that you care about.

Building a Network: Connect with people that you know. Connect with classmates, professors, past and present colleagues, and supervisors. Never burn bridges. Whether you stay in the same industry or change careers, you will need your past employers for references in the future and vice versa.

Social Media (Facebook, Instagram, Twitter, Snapchat): Always keep your personal life and work life separate. Keep these social media accounts private. If they are public, make sure that anything you post is suitable for anyone to see. Hiring managers might search for any inappropriate behavior that does not support their company's ethics. Make sure you post items that really represent you as a well-rounded candidate and person. There are some companies that want to take a look at your personal social media accounts especially if they are hiring a Social Media Manager or Marketing Manager. This is your moment to really showcase your creativity inside and outside of the office.

Passion vs. Purpose

This is a very important topic to discuss. We are molded to believe that we go to school to find our passion and that we will never work a day in our life if we find something that we are passionate about. But this concept has some flaws. Let's dig a little deeper.

Take a minute to explore your passions. What are you passionate about? Cooking, reading, art, working out? These are all passions that can be confused as hobbies, but you may not want a career in them. Write <u>all</u> of your passions on the sticky note.

Now that we have explored your passions, which one <u>serves a purpose</u>? What will make you feel <u>fulfilled</u> in the long run? That is something that you will need to brainstorm. If you're passionate about art, a fulfilling career possibility could an art teacher to high school students. Think of specific purposes when brainstorming. Why high school students? Or, perhaps you may want to open your own studio for young adults? There are some passions that you only like doing in your free time, but others that mean more that motivate you every day. Explore those differences.

Elevator Speech

This is an important step that should take some time to brainstorm. Take a look at your resume and if you do not have any work experience at the moment, you can still have one that explains your goals and your background.

Make sure to include highlights in your career that express your accomplishments. For example, if you were a marketing manager during most of your career, make sure to include your accomplishments within that time.

If you are in the middle of a career change, explain how your previous experience will translate your transferrable skill sets into the new position and how you are willing to learn something new.

If you are planning on changing careers, make sure to explain why you are seeking a change and what you find purposeful in that career that you are willing to explore.

Here are a few examples that you can model your elevator speech after. Model A is a small sample if you are seeking to continue to grow within the company or pursuing a chance to be promoted. Model B is a sample that you can use if you are switching careers. Remember to be yourself, but make sure you are able to articulate your background and your goals to the hiring manager.

I have five years of growing experience in the hotel industry working from customer service to sales, marketing & special events. I am looking for advancement opportunities within the (hotel) industry, specifically in sales & marketing, where I can take my current skill sets and apply them in a new role where I will be challenged and grow in the profession.

I have worked in the hotel industry for 5 years from customer service, to sales, to marketing, and to special events. Throughout my time in hospitality, I was able to achieve my career goals and learned valuable skill sets that I will take with me in my ongoing career, but I have outgrown my time in hotels and am looking to seek a purposeful career in education, advising undergraduate students who may have an interest in getting into the hospitality industry.

Now, it's your turn. Write your own elevator speech and practice it. Make sure it sounds genuine.

Networking

This is a necessity! Use your resources. Networking is an important tool you can use to continue to grow throughout your career. Now, we are not saying you must attend every networking event every week. Only attend those that will be valuable to you by knowing what companies will be there ahead of time. You can network within your school, current job, or online.

LinkedIn: As you continue to network, always connect with them on LinkedIn in order to keep in touch with them. They may have potential positions open in the future; many hiring managers post on LinkedIn prior to posting on their website. You can also apply directly on LinkedIn to jobs that are posted from the hiring manager.

Career Fairs: Many universities will host Spring & Fall Career Fairs. Even if you are not in the position to look for a job at the moment, attend one. This could serve as great practice for you to use your elevator speech, to get outside of your comfort zone, and to also exchange business cards. Look at potential companies that your school is connected to, learn about them, get their business card, and save it for later. Send them an email thanking them for their time and/or search for them on LinkedIn and connect with them by sending a note reminding them about a conversation you had. Check in with them from time to time. You never know, maybe job opportunity sooner than later. If sure you take a look at the list of hosting. Make sure to check if any of these they will reach out to you for a you are looking for a job, make companies that your school is companies are offering on-the-spot interviews. Do your research. Research about the company, the HR staff, the mission and vision of the company, and possible positions that they may be hiring for. Bring many samples of your resume and/or business card.

Networking Events & Communities: There are many groups or organizations within each industry for members to participate and network in. Research or ask colleagues if they belong to any organizations that you can be involved in. This can also be added to your LinkedIn profile or resume in the future!

Networking at Work: Look for an opportunity to grow. Maybe you are currently an assistant and want to be promoted within the next year or so to a management role. Look at other   departments and colleagues and research what they do. If it is something that interests you, email that person, schedule to get coffee or have lunch with them to see if they can talk about their department, their journey, and what they do. Furthermore, express your interest to know more about the department and to keep you in mind if there are opportunities in the future. Make sure to keep in touch with them. This is another way to get your foot in the door for potential management positions that may be hard to attain.

Apps: There are many online tools and apps that you can sign up for and use to network within your city. Shapr is a free app that you can download on your mobile device. It links your LinkedIn profile to the app and you can link with people within your city. Here, you can swipe right or left based on their LinkedIn profile to see if you would like to connect with that person. You can contact them to schedule a coffee, a walk, or lunch. This is a great tool for people who are new to the city or for those who are thinking of switching careers.

Congratulations! You have completed Chapter 1. You have successfully created your personal brand in order for you to move on to the next critical steps. The next steps will be formatting your resume and preparing for the interview. Are you ready?

CHAPTER TWO: LET'S GET IN PAPER FORMATION

Welcome to Chapter 2 of Nine A.M. In this section, we will dive into resume building and additional resources that will help you format your resume. Follow each step below and check off the steps as you complete each one. The following pages will also include a sample of a resume format that we recommend using. Treat this as your golden ticket to success. You got this!

Resume Building: Rough Draft

If you have a resume already started, use the following pointers to see if you already have each section and take notes of ways to strengthen them. If you do not have one, use the checklist below as a step-by-step guide for what you need on your resume in the order that it should be listed. For now, it is important that we have all of your information gathered together. Do not worry too much on the template or how it looks. Right now, let us focus on the content of your resume. We will focus on that in the next step when we finalize your resume.

Go through each step below and check off each section as you complete them on your resume. Take it step by step.

☑️ Main Sections to Include:

1. Header:

Name: Do not use various nicknames on your resume with one exception. For example, if your birth name is David but go by Dave, then you may use Dave. But do not use any childhood or friend nicknames that may ruin your professional personal brand.

Contact Number: Make sure this is always updated. If you recently changed your number, make sure you always have a resume with the most updated one. You do not want to miss an important call or career opportunity. Consider also personalizing your voicemail in case you miss a call, so they know they have reached the correct number.

Email: Use your personal email. Do not use a current or past work email. Make sure your personal email is also appropriate and easy to use. If you are a student, it is appropriate to use your university email, as long as you can still use it even after you have left school.

Address: It is always best to place your current address so employees can see that you are available for an interview or to work ASAP. If you do not feel comfortable using your personal address, make sure you at least include the city and state. Many hiring managers receive resumes from all over the world. If you just moved into the city for that specific job, this will show that you are serious about the position and are available to work if contacted. No need for them to wait on you to relocate.

2. Objective vs. Summary:

Objective: If you are a student and just starting out in your career, place a career objective. Luckily, we have done this step in the previous chapter when you brainstormed ideas about your career objectives and in formatting your LinkedIn profile. This is where you would add your career objective.

Summary: If you have five or more years of experience under your belt, include a Summary not an Objective. If you worked on your LinkedIn profile, this would be the same as the Summary section on LinkedIn. Here, you should highlight your experiences and future career objectives, in addition, be sure to list your strengths and specific tools that you are proficient in that will make you competitive, such as proficient in Workday (HR Software) or being bilingual.

3. Professional Experience:

List your previous experiences from current to past (newest to oldest).

If you are a student with little to no experience, then place internship or volunteer opportunities in this section.

Make sure to place a short description (1-2 sentences) under each company that describes that type of company. You can find some inspiration on the company's website in the "About" section.

Indicate the city and state in which each position was held. If it was a remote position, include that as well, but list the city & state of the business' headquarters.

Indicate the dates that you have worked in that company. It is best to always use a "month, year" format. If, for some reason, you had certain breaks in between multiple jobs, only indicate the "year" to avoid any awkward conversation during the interview as to why there was a huge break in between jobs. If that does come, we will discuss this further in Chapter 3, where we will dive into the interview process.

Use three or four bullet points for each position that highlights the accomplishments that you have made within that position.

Use numbers! If you managed a staff or developed an event for a company, describe the number of staff you managed and the number of attendees in that event. If you brought in sales for a company, detail how much revenue you brought in and if you increased revenue for their company. Hiring managers want to see progress and how much progress you can bring for them, if hired.

4. Education:

If you are a recent graduate, it is recommended to place this section ABOVE your Professional Experience. List the year you graduated (if you have already graduated).

If you have a few years under your belt, place this section BELOW the Professional Experience section.

Finalize your Resume: Resources & Templates

Use your resources in building a great resume; research different samples that pertain to your industry. If you are a student, consult with a career counselor on different samples that the university advises all of their students to use. Proofread your resume and ask a friend to look over it. It is important that your resume is clean and organized. Pay attention to all of the details on your resume. Not only do you need to spell check, but you also need to make sure that everything is aligned. If bullet points or certain sections are not aligned, your whole resume will look messy and convey unprofessionalism. Make sure your resume represents the fact that you are a true professional.

Hiring Managers take less than two minutes in scanning your resume. Using the wrong font or having several pages of paper that is not necessary will definitely place you in the "No" pile. In order to be placed in the "Yes" pile, make sure your bullet points are easy to read. They want to see candidates with experience or potential and if a bullet point was able to catch their eye within those two minutes, you could have a shot for an in-person interview.

University & Public Career Centers: Use your free resources. Set up an appointment with a career counselor and speak to them about career packets that they may have online or in the center. Many offices will have different resume samples that provide active verbs that you can use in your bullet points. Take advantage of your school's resources while you have it!

Apps: Take advantage of your smartphone! There are many apps designed to format your resume for you. All you need to do is type out the information and it will generate a very organized and structured resume that will stand out from the crowd.

Resume Star: Pro CV
Productivity
★ ★ ★ ★ ☆ 11 Ratings
GET
In-App Purchases

Resume Star (Free): This is a free app that can be downloaded on your iPhone. You just need to input the details for your resume in the different sections. Once you are done, it will generate all the information into a very organized resume. There are also different sample versions as well to pick from and also one to create your cover letter. It will save as a PDF that you can easily save into your Dropbox. Now, you can easily create a resume while on the go!

Pages (Free): Pages has different formats within their documents section for resumes. These templates will make sure your resume is structured and aligned. Make sure you save a PDF copy of your resume, especially if emailing or uploading. Not a lot of career websites will accept the ".docx" format and it will cause delays in the hiring process. You want to provide all hiring items needed to apply in the easiest way possible for the hiring manager.

Pages
Productivity
★ ★ ★ ★ ☆ 369 Ratings
Essentials
OPEN

Sample Resume Template:

Below is a sample template. Use this as a visual guide on how your resume should be structured.

Resume Review

Blake Smith

E: blacksmith@email.com • M: (123) 456-7890 • A: 1234 Street Rd. City, State 12345

SUMMARY

An accounting professional with 5 years of growing experience who possesses knowledge in public finance and organizational operations with emphasis on project & data management, financial analysis & reporting, fundraising, proposal writing and budgeting, event planning and communications.

- Proficient in Microsoft Office, Access, Publisher, Sales Force/Delphi, Wordpress, SquareSpace, Quickbooks, Freshbooks, Xero, NetSuite
- Possesses customer service skills, detail oriented, professional communication skills and interpersonal skills & ability to take initiative and work on multiple projects at once and under pressure

WORK EXPERIENCE

Sr. Finance Manager   MO, YR-Present
University of Atlantis, Atlantis, Indian Ocean
A premier university specializing in training students in global awareness in business, law and medicine.

- Decreased department deficits by over 50% (reduced by $100k) within the first 6 months
- Implemented new analytics and metrics based forecasting tool and processing allowing real time forecast on budgeting expenses
- Invigorated staff performance, reorganizing staff and developing talent from faculty & staff.
- Created and provide monthly financial reports, with budget reconciliations, expenditure analyses and projections & support principal investigators in developing new funding opportunities.

Finance Manager   MO, YR- MO, YR
University of Atlantis, Atlantis, Indian Ocean
A premier university specializing in training students in global awareness in business, law and medicine.

- Instrumental in financial management, including contracts, grants, and gifts and endowments, proposal preparations, budget development, contract/grant reviews.
- Consolidated all funding records and manage all data from 1995 to transform department operations towards a paperless system
- Saved $200,000 in miscellaneous expenses to increase overall department funding of successful award funding in response to private and public solicitations

EDUCATION

B.S. Business Management   MO, YR- MO, YR
University of 123, Atlantis, Indian Ocean

Now that you have completed the above steps and have a perfect resume. Take a moment to step away for a day or two. Come back to it and reread your resume. If you feel confident that this is the final draft, save it as a PDF and print it. Make sure you have it on one page (if you need 2 pages, print on both sides). Seek a Career Counselor, a peer, a colleague, a professor, or a coworker to review your resume and provide feedback.

If you feel confident your resume is ready, print and save your resume in several places. Always have an updated resume ready to go in case a hiring manager ever approaches you for an interview. Always have copies saved on a USB or backed up. You don't want to miss an opportunity if someone reaches out to you in search of a copy of your resume that they want to pass on to their hiring manager.

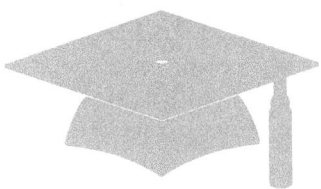

Congratulations! You have finished Chapter 2 of our Career Development Made Easy. Now that you have your perfect resume, let's help you get that job by nailing the interview process. You are almost there!

CHAPTER THREE: MAKE MONEY MOVES

Congratulations! You have made it to the final chapter. Let's put all of your hard work to use and go get that career you have always wanted. The last and final step is all about the interview process and the proper ethics and etiquette after each interview. Follow through on the steps below and you will make an impression on the hiring manager! Treat this workbook as a checklist. As you go along, check off the steps you have completed. We also provided "sticky notes" for you to take notes. Let's get started!

Preparing for an Interview:

Congratulations! They contacted you for an interview! Feeling nervous? Prepare yourself with the next few steps and you will be able to make an impression that will get you hired!

☐ Review or proofread your resume one final time

☐ Read the job description that was posted on the hiring board

☐ Read/research the company. Read up on the mission and vision statements of the company on their website. Also check out their social media pages as well.

☐ Go to glassdoor.com and read the company reviews, interview questions, and experiences that many candidates experienced for that same position you are interviewing for.

glassdoor

☐ Print out copies of your resume, references, and recommendations, or a copy of your portfolio, if needed. If you are having a panel interview, bring enough copies for everyone. Keep all materials in a professional looking portfolio with a pen and a notepad to take notes.

Write down key facts about the company that you are interviewing with on the sticky note below.

Preparing your Answers to the Interview Questions

Below are the top 10 common interview questions that are asked, along with some insight on how to answer each one. Take notes!

Tell me about yourself.

Think back to the brainstorming exercises we did in Chapter 1. Use your elevator pitch to summarize your summary and open the door as to why you are the best candidate for the job. Keep it brief, but with a lot of insight.

Name 3 strengths and 3 weaknesses.

Be prepared to name three for each. There are some interviews that will ask you to use five words to describe yourself. Research great adjectives that are not common and will make you stand out. If you use similar adjectives, make sure to back them up with an explanation.

In picking "weaknesses," keep in mind not to use the clichéd ones. Do NOT use this example: "I am a perfectionist." This example has been used over and over and hiring managers are tired of hearing similar variations of this weakness. Instead, format your answer with the following outline:

State your weakness

Define ways in which you have been proactive in honing this weakness and ways you are improving

Example: A weakness that I have experienced in the workplace is being less confident in public speaking. My previous position did not have public speaking opportunities, so I would volunteer to present or lead small team meetings in order to get practice and gain confidence. Although I am still honing my public speaking skills, I have been able to gain confidence within a year, I have put in effort as my colleagues have entrusted me to lead all team meetings moving forward.

In picking your "strengths," make sure you do not come off as "bragging." You want to remain humble and show that you are confident, but that you are also human and are able to contribute, but also learn from others.

Some companies will rephrase this and ask your greatest accomplishment. Pick an accomplishment that demonstrates how you have had a specific goal for a while and the steps you took to accomplish it.

Tell us about a time that you experienced difficulty in the workplace. How did you overcome or resolve it?

Hiring companies will phrase behavioral questions like this to gauge how you will be in the workplace.

This question can be phrased to see if you have experience working with difficult clients, customers, students, patients, etc. They want to see your customer service skills and ethics.

This question can also be phrased to see how well you will be working in a fast paced environment, working with different people, and navigating different personalities. Think of your previous experiences and how you were able to manage it. This will be a great way to showcase your interpersonal skills in the workplace.

Tell us about your work ethic.

This question is used to gauge how you work every day.

They can rephrase this question to ask about specific tools that you use to keep yourself organized.

If the job description is in need of someone organized then mention how you prioritize organization on a daily basis and mention the tools you use to keep organized.

If you introduce new tools to keep the office organized or to have better communication, that means extra brownie points for you. If you showcase that you are innovative, then you will be noticed!

Why us (name of the company)?

This is a chance for you to showcase how much you know about the company.

Bring up how your personal career goals match the company's mission statement. If you bring those goals together, this will show that you are looking at the bigger picture and not just looking for a job.

What do you know about us (name of company)?

Depending on the industry, this will be essential for you to do research on the company and/or program. Make sure you know the company, department, or program well and how it   differs from similar competing companies.

If you discuss how they are different from their competition in terms of their value, you just scored brownie points.

Why should we hire you?

This is an important question to really brainstorm. Make sure you think about your answer. You also do NOT want to repeat your career goals if you already mentioned this. Instead, use this opportunity to really sell yourself as a candidate, what you can bring to the   company, and your invested long-term interest in the company.

Showcase that you are invested in becoming an asset to the company, and that you aren't just looking for a job.

What can you contribute that other potential candidates cannot?

This is a chance for you to explain what makes you different than other candidates.

If you are a student, then this is a great chance for you to express that hiring you early will give the company an opportunity to mold you into a desirable employee instead of hiring a seasoned worker who will be harder to train.

If you are switching careers, this is a chance to express how your transferrable skills learned from your previous industry can benefit the company.

Why are you leaving your current position/ Why did you leave your past position?

This is a chance to discuss your timeline. As expressed in Chapter 2, some companies will want to understand why you have certain gaps between positions or why you may have had a shorter time at one.

If you were let go without fault for budgeting reasons, you can express that in a professional manner by explaining how the company was experiencing a financial crisis and/or was sold with many employees losing their jobs without fault.

If you are in the process of leaving your current position, you can express that there are no current positions available at the moment for you to grow into and you would like to continue to grow in a similar company.

Do not lie in any of your reasons because if they do screenings, they will find out.

Do you have any questions for us?

This is a very important question that a lot of candidates take for granted.

ASK QUESTIONS! Be prepared with at least 2 questions.

If you have questions about the position, this would be the time to ask if there was anything that you wanted to clarify.

Below are some questions that will definitely get your foot in the door:

1. What are your expectations for the candidate within the next 3 months?

2. What are the company's goals within the next 5 years?

3. What is the company/office/team culture like?

4. Think of someone in the organization who represents the right attitude for this culture. Could you tell me how they were able to exude the right attitude?

5. What is the hiring timeline for this position?

Brainstorm and write down some of your own questions based on your research on the sticky note below.

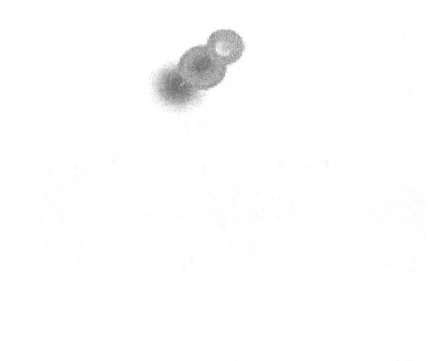

☐ Salary Negotiation

Be careful not to bring up the salary in the initial interview unless the hiring manager does. If this comes up, then be prepared on how to answer the question. Remember, you do not want to sell yourself short or look money hungry.

First, research on glassdoor.com or even linkedin.com the salary range for that position.

Second, express how your priority is finding that the position and company culture is the right fit for both parties.

Third, mention that you are being considered for positions within the $XXX-$XXX range. This way you are not selling yourself short by saying an exact number, but also letting them know that the position is within your range. It gives you room to negotiate later down the road. Based on your experience and maybe even because of the outcome of the interview, if you were able to articulate yourself well enough, some hiring managers will give you a higher salary compared to what you thought you would be offered. Go you!

☐ Tips on Communicating with Confidence

This is an important topic to discuss. Many hiring managers will look at resumes and interview similar candidates. If a candidate is perfect on paper, but does not know how to articulate themselves well, that candidate will lose the position to someone who can articulate themselves better, but who may not have as much experience as the first candidate.

If you are able to express yourself well in the interview and make the hiring manager feel comfortable with you, then they will hire you over other candidates that may have more experience.

Hiring managers want a special addition to their team. They want to make sure that any new hires will get along with them and their team, and fit in well with the company culture.

Remember, you got this, no need to be nervous! Be yourself, take a deep breath and own who you are.

The Big Day:

Here is a checklist of items you will need on the big day!

☐ Copies of Resume/Portfolio:

Remember to bring several copies to the interview. If you are attending a panel interview, ask the hiring manager who will be there in terms of the team so you are prepared to speak with 4 or 10 people. You do not want to come unprepared and be distracted by being short of one resume during the interview. You want to stay focused.

If your industry needs a portfolio, bring a copy with you for the interview. Make sure it is organized and ready to be seen.

Bring several copies of your references just in case they are ready to hire you and want to get references. Have a PDF copy ready to be emailed as well in case they ask for that.

☐ Business Attire/Appearance:

You can be the best interviewee or candidate in the world for the job, but most likely will not get hired if you do not represent yourself well. Remember, a hiring manager will only spend 10-60 minutes with you, depending on the nature of the interview. Normally, hiring managers can tell if they want to hire you within the minute they meet you. It is always best to overdress than underdress.

Ladies:

Make sure you own a business suit in neutral colors of navy blue and/or black. Make sure you have a pantsuit and a skirt version as well.

Your shoes should be work appropriate. No stilettos or boots. It would be recommended that you wear heels less than 3 inches in either navy blue or black that matches your suit. You can also wear flats if needed, but heels will always give your outfit a more formal look.

Grooming: Make sure your hair is out of your face. You do not want to spend the entire interview pulling your hair back or touching your hair. Either wear your hair up in a bun, or wear it down with a clip to make sure that any hair is out of your face. You want the hiring manager to focus on you, not your hair.

Makeup: Make sure you wear natural, minimal makeup, if you wish to. You want to look fresh the day of the interview and put together. No bright colors.

Nails: Make sure your nails are also groomed and in neutral colors. Remember your hands will be used to shake the hiring manager's hand and most likely be seen by the hiring manager if you are taking notes or have your hands in your lap.

Bags: It is essential that you bring in a professional working bag to the interview. Do not bring several bags or you will look disorganized. Bring a bag that has all of your essentials for the interview that may also hold your portfolio or resume and perhaps a water bottle. Remember to use bags that are of neutral colors.

Tattoos: Depending on the nature of the industry, it is best to cover tattoos by article of clothing, concealer, or tattoo coverage that you can buy in any Halloween or party store.

Gentlemen:

Make sure you own a business suit in neutral colors of navy blue and/or black. Make sure your belt and shoes match. Make sure button-down shirts are ironed and tucked in.

Ties: Depending on the nature of the industry, it is advised to wear a tie. Use neutral colors as well.

Make sure your shoes are work appropriate. Make sure they match your belt or are neutral colored and are polished.

Grooming: Make sure your hair is out of your face. You do not want to spend the entire interview pulling your hair back or touching your hair. Either use gel to keep your hair in place. If you have a beard, make sure that it is groomed and appears neatly, as well. You do not want to come to an interview with someone being distracted by your beard.

Nails: Make sure your nails are also groomed. Remember, your hands will be used to shake the hiring manager's hand and most likely be seen by the hiring manager if you are taking notes or have your hands on your lap.

Bags: It is essential that you bring in a professional working bag to the interview. Do not bring several bags or you will look disorganized. Bring a bag that has all your essentials for the interview that may also hold your portfolio or resume and perhaps a water bottle. Remember to use bags that are of neutral colors.

Tattoos: Depending on the nature of the industry, it is best to cover interviews by article of clothing, concealer, or tattoo coverages that you can buy in any Halloween or party store.

☐ Firm Handshake:

Practice your handshake with a peer or career counselor. Your handshake can make or break your first impression to the hiring manager.

Always extend yourself out for a handshake and make sure it is firm.

Following Up After the Interview:

Make sure to send thank you notes and to follow up after the interview!

- After each interview, within 24-48 hours, send a thank you note. Send a physical thank you note. Many people send follow up emails thanking all parties at the interview for their time, in addition to reiterating their interest and also providing their contact details once again.

- Do not nag the hiring manager. If you do so, this will only make the hiring manager not want to hire you. You have to be conscientious of their time as well in reviewing so many candidates. Follow up within a week or so if the hiring manager has not reached out. Do so by email initially and after a few days, if they have not responded, feel free to give them a call back.

Congratulations! You finished Chapter 3 of the Career Development Advising package.

Do not forget to follow us on social media, join our Facebook groups and keep in touch with the ACP team, students and parents we love to hear from you. We want to hear about your interview experience and want to be there to celebrate your success!

#knowbeforeyougo

About the Authors

Lucy Capul is a graduate of Johnson & Wales University in North Miami, Florida. Originally from California, Lucy has worked primarily in higher education serving as a Student Affairs Officer at University of California—Los Angeles (UCLA) and an Events Coordinator at University of Miami.

She currently resides in New York and is the Director of Marketing and Career Development for Affordable College Prep. Lucy enjoys helping high school and college graduates prepare for the workplace and blogs about the challenges they face. You can follow her blog, Nine A.M.- Coffee, Tea, or Snooze? at Wix.com.

Affordable College Prep is dedicated to helping college students and their families prepare for all things college. This includes tutoring, mentoring, and preparing both high school and college students for the workforce.